sashimi

THE ESSENTIAL KITCHEN

sashimi
HIDEO DEKURA

PERIPLUS

contents

Introduction 6

Japanese Knives and Sharpening 8

Utensils 10

Garnishes 14

Fish for Sashimi 18

Rectangular Slicing Techniques 20

Three-piece Filleting Technique 34

Blanching Fish: Matsukawa-zukuri 42

Tataki 46

Thinly Sliced Sashimi: Sogi-zukuri 54

Thinly Sliced Sashimi with Condiments: Hegi-zukuri 60

Paper-thin Sashimi Slices: Usu-zukuri 62

Cubic Sashimi: Kaku-zukuri 64

Cuttlefish 72

Dressed Sashimi Dishes: Aemono 82

Shellfish 92

Modern Sashimi Styles 100

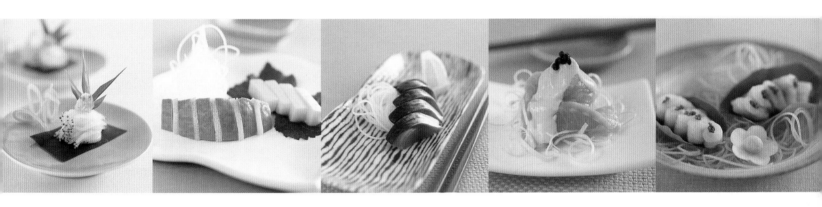

Glossary 106

Index 108

Guide to Weights and Measures 111

sashimi

introduction

Sashimi is a specialized cuisine which has developed into one of the most favored dishes around the world. In a Western meal, it makes an ideal starter. Sashimi's simple, flawless appearance masks the complex structure of its tradition and history.

Sashimi was founded during the Nara era (710-794) by the *Daizen-Shoku*, the executive chef in charge of planning and preparing the Emperor's meals. During this early period, only freshwater fish such as perch and carp were used, and it wasn't until the Edo period (1600-1868) that sashimi styles spread across Japan. New types of fish and garnishes were used, and a great diversity emerged.

Sashimi is a Japanese dish of fresh seafood fillets cut into bite-sized, oblong strips, and eaten raw with soy sauce and Japanese horseradish. While the term can be used to encompass raw beef and poultry, these are rarely eaten raw.

In Japan, konnyaku, or devil's tongue's jelly and bamboo shoots, are also used as a substitute for fish in sashimi. This book details a konnyaku recipe and introduces the concept of fruit sashimi to show that the cutting and decorating techniques can be adapted to suit several styles and food types.

Nowadays, many types of fish are used for sashimi, with the most popular being ocean fish such as tuna, yellowtail, mackerel, sea bream, and flounder. Shellfish such as shrimp (prawn), lobster, crab and abalone are also used. Shrimp are sometimes poached lightly in salted water, just enough to make them change color.

Knowing the cutting techniques for sashimi is essential, because each cutting style gives the fish fillets a different texture. It is these cutting techniques that give sashimi its delicate texture and taste. There are seven techniques presented in this book: the rectangular slicing technique, which offers two different styles of cutting, *hira-zukuri* and *hiki-zukuri*; the three-piece filleting technique, which shows how to fillet a whole fish into three pieces; the mincing technique, *tataki*, which offers two styles of grinding (mincing) fish to create texture and flavor; the thinly-sliced sashimi techniques *sogi-zukuri* and *hegi-zukuri*; the paper-thin sashimi slicing technique; the cubic sashimi cutting technique; and the cuttlefish cutting technique.

Sashimi and freshness

Always ensure that seafood is absolutely fresh when purchased. Fresh sashimi has a chunky texture and what the Japanese call *umami*, meaning the quality of tasting delicious. Overall quality is the most important aspect of selecting seafood for sashimi; while many fish can be used, not all are suitable. Because it is difficult to judge whether seafood is fresh, helpful tips are included in this book (see pages 18–19 and 92).

Over hundreds of years, the Japanese have tried various types of seafood and found cold-water species are best. Most can be consumed soon after catching, but larger fish such as tuna are best after two or three days. *Shun wa kusuri ni masaru* is an old saying that means "to eat in season is better than medicine," a belief held dear by many Japanese. Eating foods in season not only ensures the freshness of the ingredients, whether fish or vegetables, but also allows you to appreciate foods at their peak of flavor.

  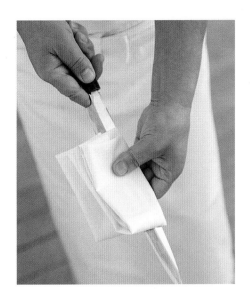

Condiments

Since its evolution during the Muromachi era (1335–1568), soy sauce (or *shoyu*) has become the dominant flavor in Japan. Its introduction changed the whole style of sashimi, from a marinated to a raw dish. Today soy sauce is an essential accompaniment to sashimi.

Soy sauce is made by fermenting soybeans, wheat malt, and brine. There are two main types, light (*usu kuchi shoyu*) and dark (*koi kuchi shoyu*). Light soy sauce is generally thinner in texture and saltier in flavor, as well as lighter in color. It can be used in dishes without darkening them. Dark soy sauce, more commonly used at the table, has a richer flavor and darker color and is slightly thicker and generally not as salty. A third type, *tamari*, is even thicker and richer and extremely dark. In Japan, it is less popular than the other two types, and is used only in the north, the Kansai region. A "sashimi soy sauce," recently developed in the Kanto region, is a lighter variety designed specifically for sashimi and is worth trying if available.

Soy sauce is produced in many Asian countries, but Japanese soy sauce is most suited to the delicacy of sashimi.

Soy sauce keeps for many months. It should be stored in a cool, dark place. Overexposure to sunlight degrades the flavor.

Condiments are used with sashimi not only for their flavor but also to aid digestion. Daikon and wasabi, the two most popular condiments, contain diastase, an enzyme that assists digestion and helps sterilize bacteria. Daikon, also known as giant white radish, is traditionally grated or shredded, then kept in cold water before serving to preserve its crispness. Daikon tastes bitter at first, but its lingering sweetness complements the flavor of raw fish. Wasabi, commonly translated as "Japanese green mustard," is green horseradish and is native to Japan. It has heart-shaped leaves that taste slightly hot. It is the root, however, that is appreciated for its intense but refreshing mustard-like flavor. The root is grated fresh or is ground into a pale green powder that is reconstituted by slowly adding water to create a smooth paste. The paste is sold in tubes or small plastic containers. Wasabi is usually served on the plate of sashimi. Soy sauce is placed in a container on the table.

Enjoy.

sharpening

ouchou, the Japanese knife, is sharper and cuts faster and sharper than Western knives. The single-edged blade, its main characteristic, is usually on the right side for right-handed use. Left-edged blades can be ordered.

There are three grades of blades in Japan: honyaki, hongasumi, and kasumi. Grading is based upon the length of time the knife remains sharp, which the Japanese call *kirehaga*. Honyaki is the highest quality, as the pure carbon steel blades retain their original sharpness for the longest period. Hongasumi and kasumi blades are both made with a combination of soft iron and carbon steel; the difference is very slight. Their softer iron outer layer facilitates sharpening.

When sharpening a Japanese knife, have a whetstone that is used with water rather than with oil. Soak Japanese whetstones in water for about 20 minutes before sharpening blades.

Sashimi knife

The yanagiba-bouchou has a carbon steel blade about 16 inches (40 cm) long. Commonly called a "sashimi knife," it is used for filleting small and medium-sized fish. A stainless steel filleting knife, about 8 inches (20 cm) long, or a chef's knife can be substituted.

Vegetable carving knife

This knife, the usuba-bouchou, is designed specifically for slicing and cutting vegetables. The blade touches the vegetable surface at a right angle, and the vegetable clings to the blade. A Western filleting knife with a stainless steel blade about 6½ inches (16.5 cm) can be substituted.

Filleting knife

The deba-bouchou, used for filleting fish, is much heavier than other knives. This weight permits a particularly sharp cut. The 16-inch (40-cm) length includes both blade and grip. This is the first knife you should purchase for preparing sashimi. Or substitute a Western filleting or paring knife with a stainless steel blade about 5 inches (13 cm) long.

Left to right: Sashimi knife, vegetable carving knife, filleting knife

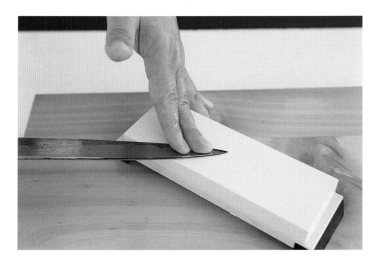

1   Place whetstone on wet towel to hold it in place. Wipe clean with damp towel and hold knife in right hand. Place top half of blade flat on stone at a 40-degree angle to the body. Placing middle and index fingers on blade, apply pressure, and move blade forward and backward. Wipe blade.

2   Once the top is sharpened, proceed to score the base of the blade.

3   As most Japanese knives are single-edged, when blades are honed the shaved pieces cling to the flat side of the blade. To remove, turn the knife, place edge of blade on corner of stone at a 45-degree angle. Slide blade down to remove excess metal.

4   Wipe knife clean with a damp towel.

Note: Steps are written for right-edged blade. Check sharpness regularly.

u t e n s i l s

Chopping board

Wooden boards are used in Japan because they grip the fish, which eases cutting and also makes it more precise. Before using the board, wet the surface and wipe with a clean cloth. Disinfect once a week by boiling and drying in sunlight. If you use a plastic board, or don't have a pot big enough to boil the board in, scrub it with salt, using a scour pad, and rinse with boiling water. For making sashimi at home, look for a board 24 inches (60 cm) square or a rectangular one measuring 18 inches by 14 inches (45 cm by 35 cm).

Mandoline

This manually operated device with a very sharp blade is used to cut vegetables such as daikon and carrot thinly and precisely. Many models have adjustable blades.

Steel chopsticks

These chopsticks are used when serving sashimi. Their weight and sharp points make it easy to handle sashimi pieces and condiments.

Tweezers

Japanese honehuki, or deboning tweezers, are heavy, with flat ends that grip bones and allow them to be pulled easily from fish. If you cannot get these, sewing tweezers can be substituted, but it is essential for ends to be broad and flat rather than pointed.

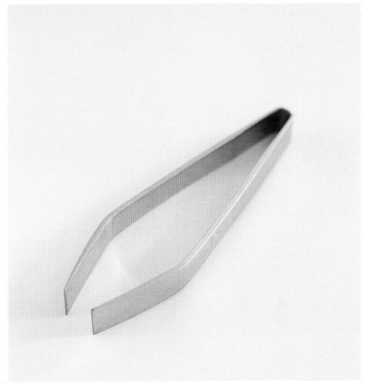

Peeler

A peeler is very convenient for removing the skin from vegetables such as daikon. It can also be used to cut vegetables into thin strips.

Grater

There are several types of graters: brass, aluminum, stainless steel, ceramic and copper. Stainless steel is recommended for making sashimi at home. The copper grater is popular with chefs for its sharp edges, but it needs to be well maintained. After each use, sprinkle grater with vinegar and brush to prevent rust. Flat or box-shaped graters can be substituted for the grater in this picture.

Vegetable cutters

Many styles of stainless steel cutters—flower shapes, leaf shapes, and various decorative shapes—are available in Japan for cutting vegetables into attractive garnishes. Outside Japan, they can be purchased at many Japanese or Asian stores.

Carving knife

There are more than fifty kinds of vegetable-carving knife world-wide, each designed to perform a particular task. Woodcraft chisels can initially be used when learning decorative carving.

Scaler

The Japanese scaler is designed so that it does not damage the flesh of a fish. A knife can be substituted for a scaler. You can use any knife to scale fish, but it is recommended that you use only the blunt edge of the knife blade. This edge won't damage the fillet. Scale from the (missing) head of the fillet to the tail, or from the wider end of the fillet to the tail end.

garnishes

Tsuma, or edible garnishes, are an essential component of sashimi. The colors and flavors are carefully chosen to complement each dish. Garnishes such as ugo (salted seaweed), shredded daikon, and shiso, an aromatic leaf from the mint family, are always used in small amounts.

Shredded daikon, one of the most popular garnishes, is traditionally prepared with a vegetable-carving knife. A mandoline can also be used. The cutting technique below can be used for many vegetables.

Shredding daikon

1   Using a vegetable-carving knife or paring knife, peel a section of daikon. Alternatively, use a peeler.

2   Placing knife at a right angle to work surface, cut daikon into very thin slices.

3   Separate slices and place in bowl of water, or refrigerate in water for 15 minutes. Drain well before using.

Carving vegetables

Vegetables such as radishes, carrots, cucumbers, turnips and potatoes, and even fruit such as watermelon, can be decoratively carved for use as garnishes. When deciding which vegetable is best suited for the sashimi you are preparing, consider the colors of other ingredients. Flowers, leaves, and other designs drawn from nature are traditionally preferred. Remember that these carved vegetables should not be the main element on the plate and therefore should not be too conspicuous. Instead, they should enhance the beauty of the sashimi.

Red radish flower

1 Make three thin cuts, spacing them evenly around radish.

2 Make three more thin cuts about ⅜ inch (1 cm) behind each first cut, making sure that the cuts meet near the bottom of the radish. Do not cut all the way through.

3 Holding bottom of radish, gently cut off the top center using tip of knife. Place egg mimosa (sieved, hard-boiled egg yolk) in middle to create the pistil of the flower.

Cucumber leaf

1 Prepare a piece of cucumber 4 inches (10 cm) long and $\frac{3}{8}$ inch (1 cm) thick, by laying cucumber on its side and cutting vertically. Place cucumber piece flat on board with skin facing up, and cut edges to create leaf shape.

2 Using tip of blade, carefully carve an upside-down "V," then another joining the ends of the first. Repeat these steps beneath the first shape. Make a smaller "V," each time ensuring blade makes only a shallow cut in cucumber flesh.

3 Insert tip of knife into side of first "V" and slice off skin, making sure to stay inside initial outline. Repeat with second "V." The white of the cucumber will contrast with the green of the skin.

Daikon flower

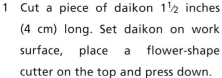

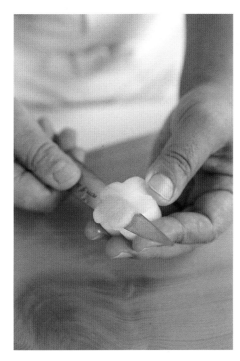

1 Cut a piece of daikon 1½ inches (4 cm) long. Set daikon on work surface, place a flower-shape cutter on the top and press down.

2 Placing the tip of the blade in the center, slice down at an angle to a 1 cm depth on the outside of the daikon. Take care not to cut past the center point. Keeping the blade in and holding the base of the daikon, spin 360°. The effect should be that the end has been cut with a pencil sharpener.

3 Repeat step 2 to make 4 flowers. Placing the tip of the blade in the center of each flower, slice 1 mm deep and spin 360°. This will ensure the center of flower is slightly sunken. Place flower upturned on board, with sunken center facing up, and place tobiko (flying fish roe), in center to create a pistil.

Note: This technique can be used to cut other vegetables, such as beets (beetroot) and carrots.

sashimi

To guarantee the freshness of fish, find a fish store or market known for having sashimi-quality fish. To determine the freshness of whole fish, make sure fish has bloodless, sparkling, crystal-clear eyes, bright pink gills, skin with a vivid color, a pleasant sea smell, and flesh that is firm and resilient to the touch.

Most saltwater fish can be eaten as sashimi. If using freshwater fish, it should be filleted and sliced, then placed in iced water immediately to tighten the texture of the flesh. Alternatively, freshwater fish can be served in citrus vinaigrette.

After purchasing fish, refrigerate as soon as possible. If you have time, clean fish and fillet to maintain its freshness. Store in refrigerator no longer than two days.

Tuna (Maguro)

Tuna is one of the most popular fish for sashimi because of its rich color and full-bodied flavor. Purchase only a block the size you need, and check that the flesh is firm.

King fish (Buri)

This fish can be found in different sizes. The 32 lb (15 kg) size is most suitable for sashimi. In Japan, the king fish is called "shusse-uo," meaning a fish whose name and texture are changed four times as it grows. If king fish is unavailable, substitute yellowtail.

Mackerel (saba)

It is economical to buy mackerel whole. Its freshness diminishes rapidly, so it must be used immediately after purchase. Mackerel is usually marinated (see recipe pages 28–29).

Bonito (Katsuo)

A relative of the tuna, bonito has red flesh and a strong taste. Combine it with a strong garnish such as ginger. It is savored as a tataki dish. Also known as skip jack.

Yellowtail (Aji)

Yellowtail is good for sashimi. With appropriate storage, it can be enjoyed within sixty hours of catching.

Salmon (Shake)

The orange color of salmon is very attractive on a plate. To store, clean, then wrap in plastic and refrigerate for up two days. If salmon is unavailable, substitute ocean trout.

Garfish (Sayori)

This small, slender fish has a long silver body and sweet-flavored flesh. Check that the body is firm. Also called Japanese half beak. If garfish is unavailable, substitute whiting.

John Dory (Matou-dai)

The clear flesh of this fish is good for paper-thin sashimi. Lemon or other citrus juices or vinegar are recommended sauces. If John Dory is unavailable, substitute lemon sole.

Lemon sole (hirame)

A whole lemon sole weighs about 2 pounds (1 kg). Autumn and winter are the best seasons for purchasing. Also known as olive flounder or common flounder.

Trumpeter (Isake)

This fish is deep bronze in color, with white lines running along its body. About 12 inches (30 cm) in length. The whole fish is usable. Also called sharp-nosed tiger fish. If trumpeter is unavailable, substitute king fish.

Cuttlefish (Ika)

Specimens weighing about 10 ounces (300 g) are good for sashimi. Look for fish with firm flesh and undamaged bodies. Avoid fish with a pink tinge. If cuttlefish is unavailable, substitute squid (calamari).

Trevally (Shimaaji)

This fish, a member of the jack family, is generally greenish on the upper half and silver on the lower. Whole fish weighing about 2 pounds (1 kg) is best for sashimi. Substitute yellowtail.

Whiting (Kisu)

The sweet-tasting, tender, fine white flesh is well suited for paper-thin sashimi (see page 62-63). It's best to purchase a whole whiting. Fillets can also be used; be sure they do not have brown markings.

Whitebait (Shirauo)

The size of matchsticks, these small silvery fish resemble shards of ice. Bones are edible.

Snapper (Tai)

Whole fish weighing about 2 pounds (1 kg) are good for sashimi. If it is kept under proper conditions, snapper can be used up to 36 hours after catching. Snapper can be enjoyed as paper-thin and blanched sashimi.

Ocean perch

Ocean perch is a Western fish. A whole fish 12 inches (30 cm) long is suitable for sashimi. This fish has shiny fins and firm white flesh. When preparing for sashimi, scale and remove skin and blanch (see page 42).

Left: Snapper; Top: garfish; Above: mackerel

S sashimi has a long history. Salt, vinegar, and then hishio were used, but it was the introduction of soy sauce that radically changed the design. Sharper knives were now used for creating slices with smoother edges, and the hiki-zukuri technique was introduced. Extremely simple, it was easy to learn. It later evolved into the hira-zukuri style, principally the same, but slightly more difficult. It is preferred by professionals as the movements are more fluid.

Hiki-zukuri

This is the easiest sashimi slicing technique. While holding a fillet in the left hand, place sharp edge of knife perpendicular to the fillet and cut into slices $1/2$ inch (12 mm) wide. When cutting each slice leave each piece in its original cut position.

Hira-zukuri

Holding a fillet in the left hand, place sharp edge of knife perpendicular to the fillet and cut into slices $1/2$ inch (12 mm) wide. While cutting each slice, slide knife from base to tip of blade in one continuous movement, then move remaining whole fillet, away from cut slices, using tip of knife. Do not push cut pieces away.

Preparing tuna block for slicing

Large fish like tuna can be purchased as a block. Tuna is roughly divided into three types of flesh: akami (red, lighter tasting part), chu-toro (medium oily part), and otoro (very oily, and expensive). Choose your favorite part of the tuna when purchasing, and as tuna can be expensive, purchase only as much as you need. Before commencing the rectangular slicing technique, trim tuna block as shown.

1   Using a sharp sashimi knife or filleting knife, trim tuna block against grain to make it uniform.

2   Cut tuna into rectangular strips about 1 inch (2.5 cm) by 2 inches (5 cm). Use leftover pieces for cubic sashimi (see pages 64–65), dressed sashimi dishes (see pages 82–83), or tataki-style sashimi (see pages 46–47).

Salmon sashimi

3 1/2 oz (105 g) ugo (salted seaweed) or shredded
   daikon

10 oz (300 g) salmon fillet without skin, bones
   removed

4 daikon flowers, for garnish (see page 17)

wasabi, for serving

soy sauce, for serving

Hints

*Use leftover salmon for cubic sashimi
(see pages 64–65) or tataki-style sashimi
(see pages 46–47).*

Rinse ugo under running water for 10 seconds to extract extra salt, then leave in cold water until needed. Slice salmon in the rectangular slicing (hira-zukuri) technique (see page 20). Place ugo on each plate and arrange 7 slices on top of ugo. Place daikon flower in middle.

    Serve with wasabi and soy sauce.

Serves 4

Tuna sashimi

12 oz (375 g) tuna block, trimmed of skin and
   dark meat

5 oz (150 g) shredded daikon

wasabi, for serving

soy sauce, for serving

Slice tuna using the rectangular slicing (hira-zukuri) technique (see page 20). Prepare 28 slices for 4 people as a main dish. Place 7 tuna slices on each plate with shredded daikon. Serve with wasabi and soy sauce.

    Placing 3 slices on the left front of plate and 4 slices on the right back is traditional in Japan.

Serves 4

Hint

Big fish like Swordfish can be substituted.

SALMON SASHIMI

Trumpeter sashimi

20 oz (600 g) whole trumpeter

3 1/2 oz (105 g) shredded daikon

8 thin lime slices, halved

4 red radish flowers, for garnish (see page 15)

1 hard-boiled egg yolk, sieved (egg mimosa)

8 chives, stemmed

wasabi, for serving

soy sauce, for serving

Fillet trumpeter into 3 pieces (see three-piece filleting technique, page 34) and remove bones. Remove skin from each piece and slice each fillet in rectangular slicing (hira-zukuri) technique (see page 20). You should have 20 slices. Place a small amount of shredded daikon on each plate and top with 5 trumpeter slices. Slip 4 lime slices between trumpeter slices.

Garnish with a radish flower. Place egg mimosa into each flower. Garnish with 2 chives. Serve with wasabi and soy sauce for dipping.

Serves 4

Hint

It is best to fillet trumpeter and remove skin just before serving. Mullet is a good substitute.

Nori tuna rolls

10 oz (300g) tuna block

4 nori sheets, halved

4 beet (beetroot) flowers (see page 17)

1³/₄ oz (50 g) shredded daikon radish

1³/₄ oz (50 g) shredded beet (beetroot)

8 cucumber leaves (see page 16)

wasabi, for serving

soy sauce, for serving

Cut tuna into cylinders 1 inch (2.5 cm) in diameter and 4 inches (10 cm) long.

Lay a halved nori sheet on board and top with 1 tuna slice. Roll up tightly using both hands. Repeat with remaining tuna slices and nori sheets. Cut each roll into 4 pieces. Divide daikon between 4 bowls. Place 4 rolls in each bowl. Garnish with beet flower and cucumber leaves. Serve with wasabi and soy sauce for dipping.

Serves 4

Hints

When slicing rolled tuna on a board, keep the board dry, or nori will become soggy. Salmon may be substituted for tuna.

NORI TUNA ROLLS

Marinated mackerel sashimi

21 oz (625 g) whole mackerel
1 tablespoon salt

FOR MARINADE
1 cup (8 fl oz/250 ml) rice vinegar or white
 vinegar
2 tablespoons sugar
1 tablespoon mirin

3 1/2 oz (105 g) shredded daikon
4 lemon wedges, for garnish
soy sauce, for serving

Fillet mackerel into 3 pieces (see three-piece filleting technique, page 34) and remove any remaining bones from each fillet with tweezers. Place fillets on a platter and sprinkle with salt. Refrigerate for 30 minutes. In a bowl, combine marinade ingredients. Remove mackerel from refrigerator and add marinade. Refrigerate for 30 minutes.

Remove mackerel from refrigerator and wipe off excess moisture with a kitchen cloth. Slice in rectangular slicing (hiki-zukuri) technique (see page 20). You should have 20 slices.

Divide daikon between 4 plates. Place 4 mackerel slices on each plate. Garnish with a lemon slice. Serve with soy sauce.

Serves 4

Hint

Yellowtail may be used in place of the mackerel.

MARINATED MACKEREL SASHIMI

Combination sashimi

3¹/₂ oz (105 g) shredded daikon

4 rectangular tuna slices (pages 20–21)

4 rectangular salmon slices (pages 20–21)

2 cucumber leaves, for garnish

2 cooked jumbo shrimp (king prawns)

3 rolled cuttlefish with okra pieces

(see pages 74–75)

2 leaf-shaped wasabi

FOR WASABI LEAVES

2 teaspoons wasabi powder

1 teaspoon water

soy sauce, for serving

Prepare ingredients just before serving. Place shredded daikon on a plate. Arrange tuna and salmon slices on opposite sides of plate. Put cucumber leaves between salmon and tuna slices. Place shrimp in front of cucumber leaves and rolled cuttlefish in front of shrimp.

To make wasabi leaves: Mix wasabi powder with water to form a smooth paste. On the plate, shape paste into 2 small ovals and, using a butter knife, shape each oval like a leaf.

Serve with soy sauce for dipping.

Serves 3

Hint

You can use kingfish or garfish as substitutes for tuna and salmon.

Konnyaku, daikon and shiso

approximately 7 oz (220 g) konnyaku
  (for sashimi)

3 1/2 oz (105 g) shredded daikon

4 shiso leaves

10 lemon slices, halved

wasabi, for serving

soy sauce, for serving

wasabi mayonnaise (see page 90)

Remove konnyaku from package, and wipe off excess moisture with a kitchen cloth. Using the rectangular slicing (hira-zukuri) technique (see page 20), slice konnyaku into 24 pieces. Divide daikon between 4 plates. Place a shiso leaf on each plate. Top with 6 konnyaku slices. Slip a lemon slice between each konnyaku slice. Each plate should have 5 halved lemon slices.

Serve with wasabi and soy sauce, or with wasabi mayonnaise.

Serves 4

Hint

If Japanese basil leaves (shiso) are unavailable, sesame seed leaves, Mitsuba leaves, or Japanese parsley can be substituted.

KONNYAKU, DAIKON AND SHISO

THREE-PIECE FILLETING
technique

Since sashimi-quality fillets are frequently unavailable, the three-piece filleting technique is worth learning. If you buy a whole fish, you can cut using this method and then refrigerate. The fish will stay fresh longer. A filleting knife with a 5-inch (13-cm) stainless steel blade is useful for filleting.

Check that your knife is sharp. If it is not, sharpen the blade before starting (see page 9). A fish with scales needs to be scaled first (see page 42). As not all fish types are suitable for sashimi, it is recommended you buy the types listed on pages 18–19. Generally, though, freshwater fish is not suitable.

Above: Bonito

1 Scale fish if scaling is required (see page 42). Using a sharp knife, slit belly of fish, remove viscera and rinse briefly. Avoid using too much tap water, as it will affect the taste. Lay fish down on board. Place knife behind gills and cut off head.

2 With one hand holding fish firmly, start cutting into the fillet from the (missing) head to the tail, along the backbone of the fish, lifting the fillet away as you cut. Place first fillet aside. Turn the fish over and repeat the process.

3 Pluck or trim away any remaining bones in the fillets or around the visceral area.

4 You should now have 3 parts: 2 fillets and 1 consisting of the skeleton and the tail. Discard skeleton and tail.

Garfish filleting

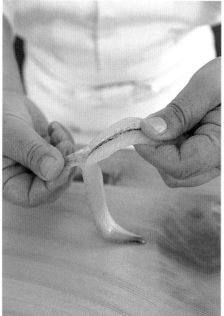

Small fish like garfish are good to work with if you are first learning how to fillet. The filleting method is quite similar to the three-piece filleting method (see pages 34–35), but is much easier.

1   Using a sharp knife, place blade behind gill and fin and cut off head. Slit belly of fish, remove viscera, and rinse fish thoroughly under running water.

2   With one hand holding fish firmly, start cutting into the fillet from the (missing) head to the tail, along the backbone of the fish, lifting the fillet away as you cut. Turn fish over and repeat process.

3   Now you have 2 fillets, and one piece consisting of skeleton and bones. Discard this as it is not edible.

4   Using fingers, peel off the skin of each fillet, from (missing) head to tail.

THREE-PIECE FILLETING TECHNIQUE

Garfish sashimi

4 whole garfish

12 small bamboo leaves, for garnish

16 capers

wasabi, for serving

soy sauce, for serving

Fillet each garfish into 3 pieces (see page 36). Remove skin from fillets. Cut each fillet along the silver center line into 2 pieces. Place 3 bamboo leaves on each plate. Roll each garfish slice and place 4 rolls on each plate. Top each rolled garfish with a caper.

Serve with wasabi and soy sauce.

Serves 4

Hint

If garfish is unavailable, whiting can be substituted.

Yellowtail, kelp and daikon rolls

4 sheets of kelp, each trimmed into 4-inch
(10-cm) squares, lighty boiled

4 whole yellowtail

4 paper-thin daikon slices, each 4 inches
(10 cm) long

2 teaspoons tobiko (flying fish roe)

nandin leaves, for garnish

wasabi, for serving

soy sauce, for serving

To boil kelp: Bring a pot of water to a boil. Add kelp and cook until tender.

To slice daikon: Using a vegetable peeler, peel 4 slices of daikon, starting from top to bottom, ensuring each slice is about 4 inches (10 cm) long.

Fillet yellowtail into three pieces (see page 35). Remove any remaining bones with tweezers. Carefully remove skin from fish with a knife. Place a kelp sheet on a board, then lay fillets on top. Roll tightly. Place a daikon slice on board, top with kelp roll, and roll tightly. Cut roll into 4 pieces. Repeat with remaining kelp, yellowtail and daikon. Divide rolls between 4 plates and garnish with nandin leaves.

Serve with wasabi and soy sauce for dipping.

Serves 4

YELLOWTAIL, KELP AND DAIKON ROLLS

Marinated garfish with kelp

4 whole garfish

FOR VINEGAR MIXTURE

$1/4$ cup (2 fl oz/60 ml) rice vinegar or
  white vinegar

1 pinch salt

1 teaspoon mirin, for seasoning

1 tablespoon water

4 dried kelp strips, each 1 inch by 8 inches
  (2.5 cm by 20 cm), rinsed

4 daikon flowers (see page 17), for garnish

4 scallion (shallot/spring onion) leaves, knotted

wasabi, for serving

soy sauce, for serving

Fillet garfish into 3 pieces (see page 36). Remove any remaining bones with tweezers. In a bowl, combine all ingredients for vinegar mixture. Soak kelp strips in mixture for 10 minutes. Place garfish fillet on board. Top with kelp strip and another garfish fillet, stacking like a sandwich. Pressing garfish and kelp with your hands, add in the vinegar mixture. Repeat with remaining garfish and kelp. Refrigerate for 30 minutes. Before serving, trim ends of each garfish and kelp sandwich neatly and cut into $3/4$-inch (2-cm) pieces. Divide pieces between 4 plates. Garnish with daikon flowers and scallion leaves.

Serve with wasabi and soy sauce for dipping.

Serves 4

Hint

When cutting garnish and kelp, wrap the sandwich

in a nori sheet to make cutting easier.

Whiting can be substituted for the garfish.

MARINATED GARFISH WITH KELP

Matsukawa-zukuri

Matsukawa-zukuri, which involves blanching, is a distinctive sashimi style. This technique has two functions: to cook the skin and outer layer of fish and to give the fish an attractive appearance. When the fish is blanched, the skin shrinks and resembles the bark of pine trees (*matsukawa*).

Fish with large scales and firm skin, such as snapper, ocean perch and silver bream, are well suited to this style.

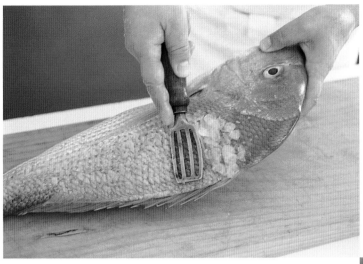

1 Scaling can be messy, so work on paper, at the sink or in a clear plastic bag. Holding head of fish and using a scaler, move scaler carefully against scales, working from tail to head. Rinse fish occasionally to make scaling easier.

2 Using a sharp filleting knife (see page 8) cut off head. Cut using the three-piece filleting technique (see pages 34–35). Place 1 fillet on a platter and pour boiling water over it to shrink the skin. Remove to a plate and refrigerate until cool. Repeat with second fillet.

3 Remove fillet from refrigerator and place on a board. Cut the fillet in half and slice in the rectangular slicing (hira-zukuri) style (see page 20).

Blanched snapper sashimi

3½ oz (105 g) cucumber

21 oz (625 g) whole snapper

8 lemon slices, halved

pesticide-free flowers, for garnish

wasabi, for serving

soy sauce, for serving

Using a vegetable peeler, remove skin from cucumber. Cut into very thin, fine strips using a sharp paring knife. Place in a bowl of cold water until using.

Remove scales from snapper (see page 42). Fillet into 3 pieces (see pages 34–35) and remove any remaining bones with tweezers. Place a snapper fillet on a platter, skin side up. Pour boiling water over fish. When skin shrinks, transfer fish to a plate and refrigerate until cold. Repeat with second fillet. Before serving, slice fish in rectangular slicing (hiki-zukuri) style (see page 20). You should have 20 pieces. Place 5 pieces on each plate. Slip lemon slices between pieces. Garnish with cucumber slices and flowers.

Serve with wasabi and soy sauce for dipping.

Serves 4

Hint

For blanched snapper sashimi, the texture is best when snapper weighs 2 lb (1 kg) or less. Larger snapper have thicker, tougher skin.

Silver Bream can also be used for blanched sashimi.

BLANCHED SNAPPER SASHIMI

t a t a k i

Originally, tataki meant beating the flesh of fish lightly with a knife to enhance the flavor. The term has expanded to include other styles, such as blanching, lightly grilling and grinding (mincing) finely, to enhance the taste of sashimi.

Lightly broiled (grilled) tataki

Bonito is suitable for this style. Before broiling (grilling), cover the fish with salt. This will make the hard skin of the bonito much easier to eat.

Blanched tataki

Blanching (see pages 42) seals the flavor of meat and fish. Tuna, swordfish and bonito are suitable for this style.

Lightly ground (minced) tataki

Yellowtail, garfish and whiting are suitable for this style. Chopping the fish with the back of the knife (not the tip) helps flavor the fish, as does the addition of other ingredients.

Ground (minced) tataki

Salmon, ocean trout and kingfish are suitable for this style. Grinding (mincing) gives fish the texture of pâté.

Marble beef tataki

FOR VINEGAR MIXTURE

$1/2$ cup (4 fl oz/125 ml) rice vinegar or white
   vinegar

1 teaspoon mirin

1 tablespoon sugar

1 white onion, finely sliced

2 scallion (shallot/spring onion) leaves,
   finely chopped

10 oz (300 g) beef sirloin (rump) block

green leaves such as bamboo or camelia leaves,
   for decoration

2 oz (60 g) grated red radish

wasabi and soy sauce, for serving

Combine all ingredients for vinegar mixture in a bowl. Place white onion in mixture. Add scallion leaves. Bring a saucepan of water to a boil. Add beef and blanch for 10 seconds. Remove beef from saucepan and add to vinegar mixture while beef is hot; toss well. Refrigerate for 30 minutes. Remove marinated beef from mixture and thinly slice (see page 54). Arrange slices in a flower shape on a plate. Place marinated white onion slices and chopped scallion in center. Garnish with leaves.

Serve with wasabi and soy sauce for dipping. Accompany with grated radish in a side plate. Each plate serves 2.

Serves 4

Hint

The beef can be broiled (grilled) rather than blanched.

MARBLE BEEF TATAKI

Lightly broiled bonito tataki

21 oz (625 g) whole bonito

¹/₄ cup (2 oz/60 g) salt, for grilling

1 white onion, thinly sliced

2 scallion (shallot/spring onion) leaves,
  finely chopped

2 oz (60 g) green ginger, grated

1 clove garlic, crushed and chopped

3¹/₂ oz (105 g) shredded daikon

4 red radish flowers (see page 15)

FOR VINEGAR MIXTURE

¹/₂ cup (4 fl oz/125 ml) rice vinegar or
  white vinegar

1 teaspoon mirin

1 tablespoon sugar

Fillet bonito into 3 pieces (see page 34) and remove any remaining bones with tweezers. Skewer 3 pieces under skin with bamboo or metal skewers. Holding fillets tightly, press salt evenly onto skin. Broil (grill) uncovered skin side of fillet, until scorched lightly. Place gently in a bowl of iced water. Rinse off salt, remove skewers from fillets, place on a plate and refrigerate for 30 minutes. In a bowl, combine all ingredients for vinegar mixture. Add sliced onion, scallion, ginger and garlic. Combine well. Remove bonito from refrigerator and slice in rectangular (hiki-zukuri) technique (see page 20). Divide daikon between 4 plates. Arrange bonito on plates. Top with onion slices and scallions. Drizzle with vinegar mixture. Garnish with radish flower.

Serves 4

Hint

Bonito in spring has a very light and subtle taste, whereas in autumn is very oily and has a remarkably deep texture. In winter, it has more fat on the flesh.

Salmon tataki

10 oz (300 g) salmon fillet, skin removed

2 chive stems, chopped

40 g ginger, grated

1 teaspoon mirin

1 pinch salt

8 shiso leaves

8 quail eggs

red maple leaves, for decoration (optional)

wasabi, for serving

soy sauce, for serving

Remove any bones in salmon with tweezers. Julienne fillet, then using a knife, chop finely with the chives and ginger. Mix in mirin and salt. Form into 8 small balls.

Cut shiso leaves in half lengthwise along the center vein and wrap each salmon ball with 2 leaf halves. If necessary, use a little water to help leaves adhere. Place 2 wrapped salmon balls on each plate. Break a quail egg in a bowl. Carefully spoon out yolk and place on top of salmon. Decorate plate, if desired, with maple leaves.

Serve with wasabi and soy sauce for dipping.

Serves 4

Hint

Ocean trout can be substituted for salmon.

SALMON TATAKI

sogi-zukuri

This sashimi style is mainly used for fish with thinner flesh, such as snapper and mackerel. The flesh of these fish types is not thick enough for the rectangular slicing techniques. The sogi-zukuri technique was developed to give the thinner slice the appearance of more width. Through the technique, a larger variety of presentation styles had the chance to develop. Thinly sliced sashimi is highly suitable for novices at eating raw fish.

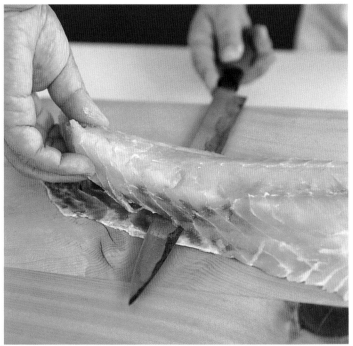

1 Scale the fish (see page 42), and fillet into 3 pieces (see pages 34–35) with a sharp sashimi or filleting knife.

2 (Above) Place fillet skin down on board, and insert knife just below the skin. While supporting fillet with left hand, gently cut parallel to the chopping board to remove skin.

3 Starting from the left of the fillet cut into diagonal slices, inclining the blade to the right at a 45-degree angle. Once the fish is cut, raise the blade to a 90-degree angle and slide each slice to the left.

Snapper with egg mimosa and tobiko

2 hard-boiled egg yolks, sieved (egg mimosa)

21 oz (625 g) whole snapper

2 tablespoons tobiko (flying fish roe)

mustard sprouts, for garnish

soy sauce, for serving

Spread egg evenly over a small baking sheet covered with aluminum foil. Place in the oven and cook egg until golden brown, about 2 minutes. Set aside.

Fillet snapper into 3 pieces (see pages 34–35) and remove any remaining bones with tweezers. Thinly slice each fillet (see page 54). Place snapper pieces and tobiko in a bowl and toss together. Add toasted mimosa and toss lightly. Garnish with mustard sprouts.

Serve with soy sauce for dipping.

Hint

Instead of flying fish roe, salted herring roe can be used. It is similar in size to flying fish roe, but light yellow and saltier.

SNAPPER WITH EGG MIMOSA AND TOBIKO

Salmon with blue cheese and white miso puree

8 oz (250 g) salmon or ocean trout fillet,
  skin removed

1³/₄ oz (50 g) scallions (shallots/spring onions),
  shredded

1 teaspoon sansho seeds (Japanese
  mountain pepper)

FOR PUREE

1 oz (30 g) blue cheese

1³/₄ oz (50 g) white miso paste

2 tablespoons mirin

1 tablespoon light soy sauce

Slice salmon thinly (see page 54). Whisk blue cheese and white miso in a bowl. Add mirin and light soy sauce. Arrange shredded scallion on 4 plates. Place salmon on the scallion on each plate and top with blue cheese sauce and sansho seeds.

Serves 4

Hint

If you prefer a lighter taste, add 1 tablespoon of sour cream to the sauce.

SALMON WITH BLUE CHEESE AND WHITE MISO PUREE   5 9

hegi-zukuri

Hegi-zukuri is the style of folding condiments such as chives, cucumber sticks, scallions, mitsuba (Japanese parsley) and cooked sliced carrot into thinly-sliced sashimi fillets. Slice a fillet in sogi-zukuri style (see page 54), then fold in half and add in the condiment of your choice.

The fish used for this style, as for sogi-zukuri, are snapper, John Dory, flounder, lemon sole, whiting and jewfish.

Right: Slice the fillet starting from left, in the sogi-zukuri style (see page 54) and prepare the condiments. Place ingredients lengthwise in center, then fold slice in half.

Lemon sole with chives

3¹/₂ oz (105 g) shredded carrot

8 taro potato leaves or large basil leaves, for serving (optional)

21 oz (625 g) whole lemon sole

1 bunch chives

4 daikon flowers (see page 17)

wasabi, for serving

soy sauce, for serving

Divide shredded carrot between 4 plates. If using, place 2 taro potato leaves on each plate, and set aside until ready to use. Fillet lemon sole into 3 pieces (see pages 34–35). Cut lemon sole fillets into thin slices (see page 54). Chop chives into 1-inch (2.5-cm) lengths. Lay a lemon sole slice on a board, and place 3 lengths of chives in the center and fold lemon sole in half. Place lemon sole on top of taro leaf. Place a daikon flower on each plate. Serve with wasabi and soy sauce for dipping.

Hint

Flounder can be substituted for lemon sole.

Serves 4

usu-zukuri

Paper-thin John Dory

21 oz (625 g) whole John Dory

½ cup (4 fl oz/125 ml) ponzu (Japanese citrus vinegar) or rice vinegar

juice of 1 lemon or 4 pieces dried or frozen yuzu

6 lemon slices, halved

16 daikon flowers (see page 17)

4 carrot flowers (see page 17)

Scale fish (see page 42) and cut into 3 pieces (see pages 34–35). Remove any remaining bones with tweezers. Then remove skin. With a sharp knife, trim left side of fillet diagonally. While holding the cut fillet with the left hand, incline the blade at a 45-degree angle to your left. Slice thinly, like paper, from the left to the right of the flesh. Slice each fillet thinly into pieces 2 inches by 1 inch (5 cm by 2.5 cm). Gently place on a plate with chopsticks or a fork. Mix vinegar and lemon juice in a small bowl. Serve vinegar sauce with sashimi. If using yuzu, put one piece into each dipping sauce bowl. Add 3 lemon slices, 4 daikon flowers and a carrot flower to each serve.

Serves 4

Hint

Plates in a color that contrasts with the fish are recommended, as the color of the plate can be seen through the paper-thin slices. If you have caviar, sprinkle over the sashimi.

Snapper can be substituted.

PAPER-THIN JOHN DORY

kaku-zukuri

Cubic cutting technique

Kaku-zukuri is a modern sashimi technique that was developed to create sashimi slices of a uniform size and thickness. This technique was designed for the specific purpose of marinating and dressing sashimi slices. The cubic thicknesss allows the outer layers of the fish to soak up the marinade flavors while the fish maintains its own flavor on the inside of the cube.

Fish with soft, thick flesh, such as tuna, salmon, king fish and bonito are suitable for cubic sashimi. Buy a block approximately 2 inches by 2 inches (5 cm by 5 cm) thick and 8 inches (20 cm) in length. A red tuna block of this size, would serve 4 people (8 pieces per person).

Cut block in half lengthwise to make two long pieces. Cut each piece in half lengthwise to make four long pieces. Then, using the hiki-zukuri cutting technique, create 1-inch (2.5-cm) cubes.

Trim tuna block into 1-inch (2.5-cm) cubes, sliding the blade along the flesh.

CUBIC SASHIMI: KAKU-ZUKURI

Tuna with yam puree

10 oz (300 g) tuna, trimmed of dark flesh and skin

2 tablespoons soy sauce

1$^3/_4$ oz (50 g) shredded daikon

3$^1/_2$ oz (105 g) yam or kumara puree

1 nori sheet, shredded

Cut the tuna into 1-inch (2.5-cm) cubes (see page 64). Place in a bowl, add soy sauce, and gently toss. Divide daikon between 4 bowls. Place tuna cubes on daikon in each bowl. Pour the yam puree over tuna and garnish with shredded nori.

Serves 4

Hint

Yam puree is available packaged from Japanese grocery stores.

TUNA WITH YAM PUREE

Blanched tuna cubes

10 oz (300g) tuna block, trimmed of dark flesh
 and skin
12 small shiso leaves or maple leaves, for garnish
pesticide-free flowers, for decoration
soy sauce, for serving

Cut tuna block into 2 pieces, approximately 1 inch by 8 inches (2.5 cm by 20 cm) or 1 inch (2.5 cm) by 6 inches (15 cm)—size of pieces will depend on size of block. Bring a saucepan of water to a boil and, using tongs or chopsticks, dip each tuna piece in water for 2 seconds. Remove immediately and place in a bowl of ice water, and refrigerate until chilled. Remove tuna from bowl, and cut into 1-inch (2.5-cm) cubes. Lay maple leaf or basil leaf over each plate. Divide leaves among 4 plates. Top with tuna cubes, cut side up. Garnish with flowers.

Serve with soy sauce for dipping.

Serves 4

Hint

Salmon can be substituted for tuna.

Bonito with egg mimosa

4 hard-boiled egg yolks, sieved (egg mimosa)

1 whole bonito, about 21 oz (625 g)

1 teaspoon English mustard or Japanese karashi

3½ oz (105 g) shredded daikon

pesticide-free flowers, for decoration

soy sauce, for serving

Preheat oven to 320°F (160°C/Gas 2½). Spread sieved egg evenly over a small baking sheet lined with aluminum foil. Place in preheated oven and cook until golden brown, about 2 minutes. Set aside.

Fillet bonito into 3 pieces (see pages 34–35), remove any remaining bones with tweezers, and cut into 1-inch (2.5-cm) cubes. Place bonito in a bowl and toss with mustard. Add cooked yolk and toss again. Divide daikon between 4 bowls. Top with bonito and garnish with flowers.

Serve with soy sauce.

Serves 4

Hint

If myoga (Japanese ginger) is available, chop 3 oz (100 g) finely and add to bonito cubes. Myoga is a crispy, juicy and aromatic condiment.

BONITO WITH EGG MIMOSA

cuttlefish

Cleaning and cutting

Cuttlefish have ink sacs and can therefore be messy to clean. As you work, be careful not to break the sac and release the ink.

Cuttlefish with a strong smell or an unusually slimy surface should not be used for sashimi.

If cuttlefish are unavailable, squid (calamari) can be substituted.

Right: Whole cuttlefish

1 Holding cuttlefish head with one hand, gently pull out shell with the other hand.

2 Gently pull out tentacles and entrails, being careful not to break the ink sac. Rinse mantle under running cold water. The tentacles can also be used for sashimi; cut them off below the eyes and remove beak. Cut tentacles into bite-sized pieces. Pour boiling water over them to blanch.

3 Slit the edge only half way on the inside of the mantle. With a firm hold, pull the skin from the edge of the fillet you have cut open. Using a cloth makes skinning easier.

Cuttlefish rolls

1 Slice cuttlefish fillet in half, stopping just at the edge (leave 1 cm of joined flesh). Gently open fillet using the blade carefully.

2 Trim off top and bottom of an okra. Prepare a nori sheet the width of one side of the opened cuttlefish fillet. Lay nori sheet on one half of the fillet and place okra in the center of the fold.

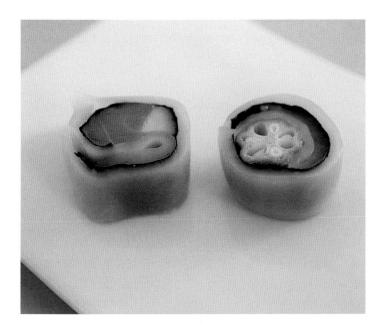

3 Wrap cuttlefish around okra and nori to form a cylindrical shape.

4 Cut into 3 pieces. Arrange, cut side up, on plate.

Left: Cuttlefish rolls

Cuttlefish rolls with okra

1 nori sheet

4 cuttlefish

4 okra

12 shiso leaves

4 carrot strips, 4 inches (10 cm) long and
  3 inches (7.5 cm) wide

4 daikon strips 4 inches (10 cm) long and
  3 inches (7.5 cm) wide

wasabi, for serving

soy sauce, for serving

Cut nori sheet into quarters, and set aside. Clean cuttlefish (see pages 72–73). Place knife blade on edge of fillet and slice in half, without cutting through. Open and lay 1 piece nori on right side. Trim ends of each okra and place 1 okra on left edge of nori sheet (closest to center) of opened fillet. Fold left side right over, then tightly roll up. Cut into 3 pieces.

Arrange shiso leaves on a plate and top with cuttlefish rolls. Holding 1 carrot strip and 1 daikon strip, tie together to form knot in center. Place on plate. Repeat for remaining servings.

Serve with wasabi and soy sauce for dipping.

Serves 4

Hint

Buy okra that is young and tender. As a substitute for okra, salmon slices, tuna slices, pickled ginger and sliced cucumber can be used.

CUTTLEFISH ROLLS WITH OKRA

Julienned cuttlefish sashimi

2 cuttlefish

1 teaspoon sake

2 tablespoons tobiko (flying fish roe)

1 hard-boiled egg yolk, sieved (egg mimosa)

1 scallion (shallot/spring onion) leaf, about 4
  inches (10 cm) long, julienned lengthwise

soy sauce, for serving

Clean cuttlefish (see pages 72–73), and julienne fillets. Place in a bowl and sprinkle with sake. Add tobiko and mix to combine. Divide between 4 bowls and sprinkle with sieved yolk. Slice scallion leaf into 4 thin strips and garnish cuttlefish.

Serve with soy sauce for dipping.

Serves 4

Cutting julienne strips

Cuttlefish and squid (calamari) are slippery. Be careful when slicing. After cleaning cuttlefish (see pages 72–73), place fillet on board and use tip of knife to slice in julienne strips.

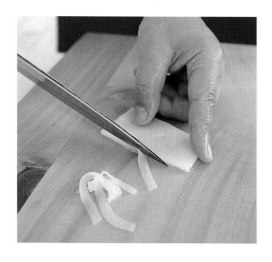

Hint

If cuttlefish is unavailable, squid (calamari) can be substituted. Peel off outer skin layer of squid before eating raw.

JULIENNED CUTTLEFISH SASHIMI

Blanched cuttlefish with ao-nori

4 cuttlefish

1 tablespoon ao-nori (flaked green nori)

4 lemon wedges

pine sprigs, for decoration

soy sauce, for serving

Clean cuttlefish (see pages 72–73), and cut in half vertically. Place 1 piece at a time, outside surface down, and score inside vertically, spacing scoring every $\frac{1}{4}$ inch (6 mm). Turn 90 degrees and score again, making a crosshatch pattern. Refrigerate until cooled. Take out and place in the center of a plate, then sprinkle with ao-nori. Place pine sprigs on one side of the cuttlefish. Garnish with a wedge of lemon.

Serve with soy sauce.

Serves 4

Hint

If ao-nori is unavailable, chopped chives can be substituted.

aemono

Combining sashimi with condiments or sauces adds flavor. Strong-flavored fish, such as bonito, yellowtail and garfish, also benefit from this style.

You can create an enormous range of dressed dishes using the many varieties of sashimi fish, the different slicing techniques, and the numerous condiments and sauces.

Four slicing techniques are most suitable: cubic, thin slice, paper-thin slice and julienne slice. Tataki-style sashimi can also be dressed with condiments and sauces.

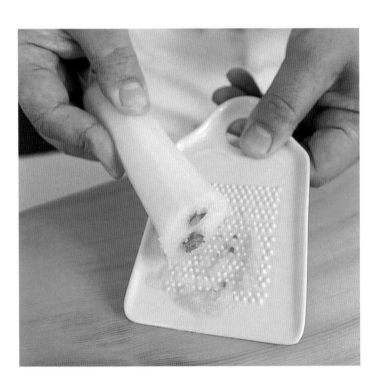

Grated chili and daikon
Momiji-oroshi

7 oz (220 g) daikon

2 small red chili peppers

Peel daikon and trim ends. Make 2 small holes in ends with chopsticks, large enough for a chili pepper. Insert 1 chili into each hole. Grate daikon and mix gently in a bowl.

The combination of hot chili and bitter daikon refreshes the palate and is especially suited to light-tasting sashimi, such as usu-zukuri (paper-thin sashimi) with a vinaigrette sauce. It is particularly good for white-fleshed fish.

Serves 4

Green tea miso
Maccha miso

1 tablespoon maccha (green
tea powder)

1¹/₂ teaspoons white miso

2 teaspoons mirin

In a bowl, mix tea powder, miso and mirin, and whisk together until well combined.

Serves 4

Black sesame paste
Goma-dare

¹/₄ cup black sesame seeds,
toasted

2 tablespoons mirin

1 teaspoon green-ginger juice

Grind sesame seeds, using a mortar and pestle, gradually adding mirin and green-ginger juice. Mix until smooth. Use as an accompaniment to steamed sashimi.

Serves 4

Egg-yolk vinaigrette
Kimizu

4 egg yolks, beaten

1 tablespoon rice vinegar

1 teaspoon mirin

In a bowl, whisk egg yolk and rice vinegar. Add mirin and whisk together. Sieve mixture well. Egg-yolk vinaigrette is used as a dressing or as a dipping sauce for sashimi slices made with white-fleshed fish, such as snapper, silver bream and John Dory.

Serves 4

Marinated yellowtail

1 yellow (brown) onion

4 whole yellowtail

1²/₃ oz (50 g) green ginger, grated

1 clove garlic, crushed

1 scallion (shallot/spring onion) stem, finely
  chopped

4 shiso leaves

2 myoga, halved

3¹/₂ oz (100 g) shredded daikon

4 red radish baskets with wasabi

²/₃ oz (20 g) wasabi

FOR VINEGAR MIXTURE

¹/₂ cup (4 fl oz/125 ml) rice vinegar

2 tablespoons sugar

1 pinch salt

1 teaspoon mirin

Slice onion. Place slices in a bowl of ice water. Fillet yellowtail (see page 36) and cut into small squares, approximately ³/₈ inch (1 cm) wide. Drain sliced onion.

In a bowl, add all vinegar ingredients and mix until well combined.

Place sliced onion, grated ginger, crushed garlic and chopped scallion in a bowl. Pour in vinegar mixture and mix using chopsticks or a fork. Add yellowtail pieces and mix gently. Remove pieces and place on a board, then lightly grind (mince) with the back of a knife blade to absorb the flavor (see Lightly ground tataki page 47). Lay a shiso leaf on each plate or bowl with crushed ice, then arrange yellowtail pieces on each plate or bowl, and top with condiments from the vinegar mixture. Garnish with a half myoga leaf and 1 radish basket, per plate.

Serves 4

Hint

Bonito is also suitable for this dish.

Ocean perch with plum puree

10 oz (300 g) whole ocean perch

3 1/2 oz (100 g) plum puree

1 shiso leaf, finely chopped

1 shiso leaf, julienned

1 3/4 oz (50 g) shredded daikon

Scale fish (see page 42) and fillet into 3 pieces (see pages 34–35). Remove any remaining bones with tweezers. Broil (grill) fillets lightly on skin side only, over direct fire or on an uncovered broiler (grill) until the skin just changes color. Then slice in hiki-zukuri style (see page 20). Mix the plum puree and chopped shiso leaves together. Divide shredded daikon between four plates. Arrange sliced fish on each plate, and top with puree. Sprinkle with julienned shiso.

Serves 4

Hint

Jewfish or baby snapper can be substituted.

OCEAN PERCH WITH PLUM PUREE

Snapper with grapefruit and emerald sauce

7 oz (220 g) snapper fillet, skin removed

1 grapefruit

2 kiwifruits

4 mint leaves, for decoration

Slice snapper fillet into 24 pieces, using the *sogi-zukuri* technique (see page 54). Cut off ends of grapefruit. Stand on a board and slice off peel and rind. Remove all white pith. Holding grapefruit, cut into 8 sections, removing rind between sections.

Peel kiwifruits, and puree in blender. Place about 6 snapper slices on each plate and top with 2 grapefruit pieces. Drip kiwifruit puree around fish with a teaspoon. Top with mint leaf.

Serves 4

Hint

Jewfish and lemon sole can be substituted.

Crabmeat with wasabi mayonnaise

1 tablespoon sake

1 tablespoon salt

8 fresh Alaskan (snow) crab sticks

ice water, for chilling

4 strips of daikon 4 inches by $1/2$ inch
  (10 cm by 12 mm)

16 long chives, stemmed

$1/4$ punnet mustard cress

FOR WASABI MAYONNAISE

$1^3/4$ oz (50 g) light mayonnaise

$1/3$ oz (10 g) wasabi

Bring a pot of water to a boil and add sake and salt. Wrap the sticks of crab meat with a cotton cloth, and tie so they don't come apart, then boil. When cloth floats to the surface, remove crab and place in iced water. Unwrap the crab legs once they have cooled.

Mix wasabi and mayonnaise to a smooth consistency. Cut each crab stick in half. Tie 2 crab sticks together with 4 pieces chives. Place a tied crab stick to stand on cut end on each bowl, and top with wasabi mayonnaise, daikon strip and mustard cress.

Serves 4

Hint

Lobster meat can be substituted for crabmeat.

CRABMEAT WITH WASABI MAYONNAISE

shellfish

Shellfish deteriorates rapidly, so you need to buy live or precooked specimens. If you buy a live shellfish and wish to keep it fresh overnight, wrap with newspapers and place in the refrigerator. Check when you purchase for the best season in which to buy shellfish.

Abalone

This is a favored but expensive shellfish. It has cream-colored flesh with a mild flavor. Fresh abalone will live for several days, if you keep it in a cool place in a sack soaked in salt water.

To make the flesh firm, spread with salt. Then stand for about 10 minutes. With a butter knife, remove flesh from shell, and rinse. Discard mantle (frill) with a sharp knife (a sashimi or filleting knife). Trim and slice in sogi-zukuri style (see page 54). If you cannot purchase live abalone it is recommended that you eat it cooked.

Sea urchin

Sea urchin is a great treat, and a delicacy in Japan. It has an unusual fresh sea smell and smooth texture. Moreover, the smell and texture go very well with sake or wine.

You can try to open the prickly shell of a sea urchin with a knife or you can purchase the orange-yellow ovaries from a market. Chose firm, fresh-colored ovaries.

When opening prickly shell, wear gloves. Using a sturdy knife, cut the shell in half on a board. Open shell without cutting eggs. Scoop out eggs with a knife or spoon. Serve with wasabi and soy sauce.

Scallops

A large bivalve, up to 8 inches (20 cm) across, the scallop is especially prized for its tender flesh, which makes delicious sashimi.

Purchase scallops in the shell. After removing from the shell, rinse in salted water. Since the veins and roe have a strong fishy flavor, discard them. Slice in sogi-zukuri style (see page 54) and serve with wasabi and soy sauce. Lemon juice is also recommended for dipping. If only scallops for cooking are available, blanch them before making sashimi.

Oysters

It's best to purchase oysters in the winter because glycogen, which is the natural flavor enhancer, is increased. Buy oysters that are oily and have puffy flesh. Shuck oysters (see page 94) and eat them immediately after purchasing. Oysters are rich in minerals and vitamins.

Clockwise from top left:
Oyster, sea urchin, scallop

Kaki-oyster cocktail

3 cups (24 fl oz/750 ml) water

1 tablespoon salt

8 oysters

2 nori sheets, quartered

4 tablespoons grated chili and daikon
   (see page 82)

1 tablespoon tobiko (flying fish roe)

8 chive stems, halved

$1^3/_4$ oz (50 g) ugo (salted seaweed)

$1^3/_4$ oz (50 g) shredded daikon

FOR VINAIGRETTE MIXTURE

2 tablespoons rice vinegar

1 teaspoon sugar

$^1/_2$ teaspoon mirin

2 drops soy sauce

Combine all ingredients for vinaigrette mixture in a bowl. Set aside. Place water in bowl and stir in salt.

To shuck oysters: Using an oyster opener or a butter knife, hold oyster in palm of one hand and insert knife into the shell where it is joined together like a hinge. Push against the hinge and twist knife to open shells.

Dip oysters in salted water to enhance texture. Shape each piece of nori into a cylinder and seal using water. Place oyster in cylinder and cylinder in oyster shell. Place grated chili and daikon in shell. Arrange tobiko between daikon and oyster. Insert 2 chive stems in tobiko. Arrange ugo and shredded daikon in the center of each plate. Top with the oyster cocktail in the center of ugo and daikon bed. Drizzle with vinaigrette mixture.

Serves 4

Hint

Chose plump and lustrous oysters with a fresh smell.

KAKI-OYSTER COCKTAIL

Sea urchin

$1/2$ nori sheet

1 English (hothouse) cucumber

$5^1/_4$ oz (155 g) sea urchin roe

8 kinome (Japanese pepper) sprigs or daikon
  sprouts

wasabi, for serving

soy sauce, for serving

Cut nori sheet in half. Dip cucumber in water. Place cucumber on nori sheet and roll tightly. Trim both sides of cucumber ends so cucumber does not protrude from roll, then cut roll into 8 pieces.

Place 2 slices of sea urchin roe on cut side of cucumber roll, and top each sea urchin with kinome. Place 2 cucumber rolls in each bowl and serve with wasabi and soy sauce.

Serves 4

Scallop sashimi

8 scallops

3 cups (24 fl oz/750 ml) salt water

1 tablespoon salt

4 tablespoons salmon caviar

FOR GREEN TEA MIXTURE

1 tablespoon green tea powder

1 tablespoon white miso

1 teaspoon mirin

Rinse scallop shells before using. Insert butter knife in shell and open. Do not discard remaining shells, as they will be used for presentation.

Cut out meat and place in a bowl and add salt. Dip scallops in salted water. In another bowl, combine all ingredients for green tea mixture. Divide tea mixture between 4 half-shells. Place 2 scallops in each shell. Top with caviar.

Serves 4

Hint

Abalone can be substituted for scallops.

SCALLOP SASHIMI

styles

Whitebait sashimi

$^1/_4$ cup (2 fl oz/60 ml) rice vinegar

4 kelp sheets, 1 inch by 4 inches (2.5 cm by 10 cm)

10 oz (300 g) whitebait

1 tablespoon mirin

4 carrot strips (with peeler, peel 20 cm/
8 inches long)

4 bamboo sprigs, for decoration

wasabi, for serving

soy sauce, for serving

Bring saucepan of salted water to a boil. Place rice vinegar in a bowl. Dip kelp sheets in boiling water. Remove and place in rice vinegar. Top with whitebait, and sprinkle with mirin. Arrange a carrot strip and a bamboo sprig.

Serve with wasabi and soy sauce.

Serves 4

Hint

Small shrimp (prawns) can be substituted.

WHITEBAIT SASHIMI

Sashimi in lime baskets

4 large limes

4 thin slices snapper

4 okra slices

4 cooked jumbo shrimp (king prawns)

4 salmon strips, 1 inch (2.5 cm) long

4 nori squares 1¼ inch by 1¼ inch
   (3 cm by 3 cm)

bamboo sprigs

pesticide-free flowers, for decoration

With a small knife or zester, remove narrow strips of peel from lime, working end to end. Cut blossom end of each lime, creating a lid. Scoop out lime with a spoon, leaving a shell. Roll up a snapper piece and place in each basket, then top with an okra slice. Insert a cooked shrimp in basket. Roll salmon strip with nori and trim, then place in basket. Decorate with a bamboo sprig and a flower.

Serves 4

SASHIMI IN LIME BASKETS

Avocado and papaya sashimi

1 ripe but firm avocado

5 oz (150 g) papaya (paw paw)

4 oz (125 g) shredded daikon

8 shiso leaves

10 lemon slices, halved

FOR WASABI MIXTURE

1 tablespoon wasabi

2 tablespoons light soy sauce

1 tablespoon mirin

Slice avocado in half, remove pit, and peel. Cut each half in half lengthwise. Slice avocado in rectangular (hiki-zukuri) style (see page 20).

Cut papaya in half and remove seeds. Cut each half in half lengthwise, using the same style as avocado.

Divide shredded daikon between 4 plates, and place 2 shiso leaves on each plate. Sandwich lemon slices between avocado and papaya slices and 1 section of avocado slices on shiso leaves. In a bowl, combine all ingredients for wasabi mixture.

Serve as a side dish with other sashimi.

Serves 4

Glossary

Ao-nori: Edible green seaweed. Sold in dried flake form. It is usually sprinkled when served, so it is not too moist when eaten.

Bamboo leaves: Inedible garnish, often used when fish is placed on top of leaf. Bamboo leaves need sustained moisture and should be kept in water until needed.

Chives: Slender onion-flavored herb. The leaves and stems are chopped and used to flavor or decorate sashimi.

Daikon: White horseradish with a slightly hot flavor.

Egg mimosa: Sieved egg yolk cooked until hard (hard-boiled), used for sprinkling or a decoration such as the stamen in a carved radish flower. To make a teaspoon of egg mimosa, place a fresh egg in a pot of water. Bring water to a boil and simmer for 15 minutes until egg is hard-boiled. Remove egg shell under running water and when egg is chilled, remove egg white. Place egg yolk in a sieve. Pressing with a teaspoon, sieve into a small bowl.

Green-ginger juice: Peel a green ginger and grate into a bowl. Squeeze with fingers to make green-ginger juice.

Ginger (fresh): Grated fresh ginger has a hot and spicy taste, and is used as flavoring for marinade sauces.

Julienned: Cut into thin strips like matchsticks.

Karashi: Karashi is similar to English mustard, but hotter.

Kelp: Large dark brown seaweed sold dry. When using, rinse kelp and soak in water. Kelp is highly nutritious, but it is seldom eaten on its own. The umami (deliciousness) element in kombu (dried kelp) enhances the taste of dishes.

Kinome: Japanese pepper; the sprigs provide an aromatic additional flavor. They are an edible garnish or herbal ingredient. May be chopped or used as a pâté.

Konnyaku: Devil's tongue jelly. Made from konnyaku potato and formed either into bricks or strings, which are usually used for cooked dishes.

Maccha: Green tea, a green powdered tea with a bitter yet pleasant taste. This tea is indispensable in a Japanese tea ceremony.

Mirin: Sweet rice wine for cooking. Made by mixing steamed glutinous rice and malt, containing 10–14% alcohol. Sugar can be substituted for mirin, but mirin has a milder sweetness when mixed with other condiments.

Miso: Made by fermenting soybean paste and wheat barley or rice. Full of protein. White miso has a lighter taste and less salt. Usually used in dressings or as sauce for sashimi. Better to use with blue cheese puree because of its contrasting color. A few tonal variations are available. The cream tone is quite easy to find at most Japanese Asian food stores.

Myoga: Japanese ginger, but has quite a different herbal fragrance than ginger when sliced thinly as a sashimi condiment.

Nandin leaves: An evergreen shrub. Originating in China, it can grow approximately 6 feet (2 m). Each sprig has 3 or more leaves, the shape of a small feather. In winter, the small white petals change into red inedible fruit. In Japan, this plant is favorable as a garden plant. Furthermore, it is often used as the symbol in family crests.

Nori: Edible seaweed in dark brown and deep green dried sheets. Standard size is 8 inches by 7 inches (20 cm by 17 cm). Sold in packets of ten. Small-sized nori is also available.

Okra: Vegetable with green seed pods. Sliced okra has the appearance of a star or snow flake, good for decorative garnishes. Fresh okra has a sticky texture that is good with sashimi.

Rice vinegar: Vinegar fermented from rice, and fairly mild in flavor. Rice is the staple food of the Japanese, and rice vinegar matches sushi rice and other dishes perfectly.

Sake: Japanese rice wine. Produced by brewing rice. Taste ranges from dry to sweet. Can be drunken chilled, at room temperature, or warmed. After opening, refrigerate with a cap on the bottle; can be enjoyed for a couple of months.

Sansho: Japanese pepper, bitter tasting. Sansho is usually bought ground, since it keeps its aroma well. Usually, sansho seeds are sold after being cooked with soy sauce, sugar, kelp stock and other ingredients.

Scallion (shallot/spring onion): Tasting similar to onion, this vegetable has a thin white bulb and green stem.

Tobiko: Preserved flying fish roe. A very thin texture, and a sparkling orange color.

Ugo: Salted green seaweed, sold in a packet. Before using, rinse well.

Ume-boshi: Dried, salt-pickled Japanese plum, colored with red shiso (Japanese basil). As it is quite salty, use a tiny amount.

Wakame: Dark brown edible seaweed, thinner than kelp. Used for garnish for sashimi. Dried wakame must be soaked before using.

Yam (hairy mountain yam or kumara): When peeled and finely grated, it has a gluey consistency, and looks like melted cheese or very thick cream. It has excellent digestive qualities. It is eaten in its gluey form with soy sauce or with vegetables, fish, cooked rice, and other ingredients such as thickened sauce. When making Japanese pancakes, add yam powder to flour mixture to make the pancakes puffy.

Yuzu (Japanese citron): Yuzu is used mostly for its zesty aroma. Dried, powdered or frozen yuzu are available all year round from Japanese grocery stores.

Index

A

Abalone, description of 92
Aemono 82–84
Ao-nori
    with blanched cuttlefish 80
    description of 106
Avocado and papaya sashimi 104

B

Bamboo leaves 106
Beef tataki, marble 48
Black sesame paste 83
Blanched cuttlefish with ao-nori 80
Blanched snapper sashimi 44
Blanched tataki 46
Blanched tuna cubes 68
Blanching technique 42
Blue cheese and white miso puree
    with salmon 58
Bonito
    description of 18
    with egg mimosa 70
    lightly broiled tataki 50
Broiled bonito tataki 50
Broiled tataki 46

C

Carving knives 13, 8
Carving vegetables 15–17
Cheese, blue, and white miso puree
    with salmon 58
Chili and daikon, grated 82
Chives 106
Chopping board 10
Chopsticks, steel 10

Citron, Japanese 107

Citron, Japanese 107
Combination sashimi 30
Condiments 7. see also Dressings
Crabmeat with wasabi mayonnaise 90
Cubic cutting technique 64
Cucumber leaf 16
Cuttlefish
    blanched, with ao-nori 80
    cleaning and cutting 72–73
    description of 19
    julienned sashimi 78
    rolls 74–75
    rolls with okra 76

D

Daikon
    and chili, grated 82
    description of 106
    flower 17
    konnyaku and shiso 32
    shredding 14
    yellowtail and kelp rolls 38
Dressings
    black sesame paste 83
    egg-yolk vinaigrette 83
    grated chili and daikon 82
    green tea miso 83

E

Egg mimosa
    with bonito 70
    description of 106
    and tobiko with salmon 56
Egg-yolk vinaigrette 83

F

Filleting
    garfish 36
    knife 8
    three-piece technique 34

G

Garfish
    description of 18
    filleting 36
    marinated, with kelp 40
    sashimi 37
Garnishes 14–17
Ginger 106
Goma-dare 83
Grated chili and daikon 82
Grater 12
Green-ginger juice 106
Green tea miso 83
Grilled tataki 46
Ground tataki 47

H

Hegi-zukuri slicing technique 60
Hiki-zukuri slicing technique 20
Hira-zukuri slicing technique 20

J

John Dory
    description of 18
    paper-thin 62
Julienne
    cuttlefish sashimi 78
    description of 106

K

Kaki-oyster cocktail 94
Kaku-zukuri slicing technique 64
Karashi 106
Kelp
    description of 106
    marinated garfish with 40
    yellowtail and daikon rolls 38
Kimizu 83
King fish, description of 18
Kinome 106
Knives
    filleting 8
    sashimi 8
    sharpening 9
    vegetable carving 13, 8
Konnyaku
    daikon and shiso 32
    description of 106

L

Lemon sole
    with chives 60
    description of 18
Lightly broiled bonito tataki 50
Lime baskets, sashimi in 102

M

Maccha
    description of 106
    miso 83
Mackerel
    description of 18
    marinated sashimi 28
Mandoline 10
Marble beef tataki 48
Marinated garfish with kelp 40
Marinated mackerel sashimi 28
Marinated yellowtail 84
Matsukawa-zukuri blanching
    technique 42

Mayonnaise, wasabi 90
Minced tataki 47
Mirin 106
Miso
    description of 106
    green tea 83
    puree, white, with blue cheese and
        salmon 58
Momiji-oroshi 82
Myoga 106

N

Nandin leaves 106
Nori
    with blanched cuttlefish 80
    description of 107
    tuna rolls 26

O

Ocean perch
    description of 19
    with plum puree 84
Okra
    with cuttlefish rolls 76
    description of 107
Oysters
    description of 92
    kaki cocktail 94

P

Papaya and avocado sashimi 104
Peelers 11
Perch, ocean
    description of 19
    with plum puree 84

R

Radish flower 15
Red radish flower 15
Rice vinegar 107

Rolls
    cuttlefish 74–75
    cuttlefish, with okra 76
    nori tuna 26
    yellowtail, kelp and daikon 38

S

Sake 107
Salmon
    with blue cheese and white miso
        puree 58
    description of 18
    sashimi 22
    tataki 52
Sansho 107
Sauces see Dressings
Scalers 13
Scallion 107
Scallops
    description of 92
    sashimi 98
Sea urchin
    description of 92
    sashimi 96
Sesame paste, black 83
Shallot 107
Sharpening knives 9
Shellfish 92
Slicing techniques
    hegi-zukuri 60
    hiki-zukuri 20
    hira-zukuri 20
    kaku-zukuri 64
    sogi-zukuri 54
    usu-zukuri 62
Snapper
    blanched, sashimi 44
    description of 19
    with egg mimosa and tobiko 56
    with grapefruit and emerald
        sauce 88

Sogi-zukuri slicing technique 54
Sole, lemon
    with chives 60
    description of 18
Soy sauce 7
Spring onion 107
Steel chopsticks 10

T

Tataki 46–47
Three-piece filleting technique 34–35
Tobiko
    description of 107
    with snapper and egg mimosa 56
Trevally, description of 19
Trumpeter
    description of 19
    sashimi 24
Tsuma 14–17
Tuna
    blanched cubes 68
    description of 18
    nori rolls 26
    preparing for slicing 21
    sashimi 22
Tuna with yam puree 66
Tweezers 11

U

Ugo 107
Ume-boshi 107
Usu-zukuri slicing technique 62
Utensils 10–13

V

Vegetables
    carving 15–17
    carving knife 8, 13
    cutters 12
Vinaigrette, egg-yolk 83

W

Wakame 107
Wasabi
    leaves 30
    mayonnaise 90
Whitebait
    description of 19
    sashimi 100
Whiting, description of 19

Y

Yam
    description of 107
    puree with tuna 66
Yellowtail
    description of 18
    kelp and daikon rolls 38
    marinated 84
Yuzu 107

Guide to weights and measures

The conversions given in the recipes in this book are approximate. Whichever system you use, remember to follow it consistently, thereby ensuring that the proportions are consistent throughout a recipe.

WEIGHTS

Imperial	Metric
1/3 oz	10 g
1/2 oz	15 g
3/4 oz	20 g
1 oz	30 g
2 oz	60 g
3 oz	90 g
4 oz (1/4 lb)	125 g
5 oz (1/3 lb)	150 g
6 oz	180 g
7 oz	220 g
8 oz (1/2 lb)	250 g
9 oz	280 g
10 oz	300 g
11 oz	330 g
12 oz (3/4 lb)	375 g
16 oz (1 lb)	500 g
2 lb	1 kg
3 lb	1.5 kg
4 lb	2 kg

USEFUL CONVERSIONS

1/4 teaspoon	1.25 ml
1/2 teaspoon	2.5 ml
1 teaspoon	5 ml
1 Australian tablespoon	20 ml (4 teaspoons)
1 UK/US tablespoon	15 ml (3 teaspoons)

Butter/Shortening

1 tablespoon	1/2 oz	15 g
1 1/2 tablespoons	3/4 oz	20 g
2 tablespoons	1 oz	30 g
3 tablespoons	1 1/2 oz	45 g

OVEN TEMPERATURE GUIDE

The Celsius (°C) and Fahrenheit (°F) temperatures in this chart apply to most electric ovens. Decrease by 25°F or 10°C for a gas oven or refer to the manufacturer's temperature guide. For temperatures below 325°F (160°C), do not decrease the given temperature.

VOLUME

Imperial	Metric	Cup
1 fl oz	30 ml	
2 fl oz	60 ml	1/4
3	90 ml	1/3
4	125 ml	1/2
5	150 ml	2/3
6	180 ml	3/4
8	250 ml	1
10	300 ml	1 1/4
12	375 ml	1 1/2
13	400 ml	1 2/3
14	440 ml	1 3/4
16	500 ml	2
24	750 ml	3
32	1L	4

Oven description	°C	°F	Gas Mark
Cool	110	225	1/4
	130	250	1/2
Very slow	140	275	1
	150	300	2
Slow	170	325	3
Moderate	180	350	4
	190	375	5
Moderately Hot	200	400	6
Fairly Hot	220	425	7
Hot	230	450	8
Very Hot	240	475	9
Extremely Hot	250	500	10

First published in the United States in 2001 by Periplus Edition (HK) Ltd.,
with editorial offices at 153 Milk Street, Boston, Massachusetts 02109 and
5 Little Road #08-01 Singapore 536983

Library of Congress Cataloguing-in-Publication Data is available.
ISBN 962-593-935-0

DISTRIBUTED BY

North America
Tuttle Publishing
Distribution Center
Airport Industrial Park
364 Innovation Drive
North Clarendon, VT 05759-9436
Tel: (802) 773-8930
Fax: (802) 773-6993

Japan
Tuttle Publishing
RK Building, 2nd Floor
2-13-10 Shimo-Meguro, Meguro-Ku
Tokyo 153 0064
Tel: (03) 5437-0171
Fax: (03) 5437-0755

Asia Pacific
Berkeley Books Pte Ltd
5 Little Road #08-01
Singapore 536983
Tel: (65) 280 3320
Fax: (65) 280 6290

Set in Frutiger on QuarkXPress
Printed in Singapore

First Edition
06 05 04 03 02 01 10 9 8 7 6 5 4 3 2 1